THE
JACKSONS

THE

JACKSONS

BY STEVE MANNING

PHOTOGRAPHS BY KWAME BRATHWAITE

THE BOBBS-MERRILL COMPANY, INC.
INDIANAPOLIS / NEW YORK

Copyright © 1976 by Steve Manning
Photographs © 1976 by Kwame Brathwaite

All rights reserved, including the right of reproduction in whole or
in part in any form
Published by the Bobbs-Merrill Company, Inc.
Indianapolis   New York

Designed by Jerry Byers
Manufactured in the United States of America

Library of Congress Cataloging in Publication Data

Manning, Steve.
  The Jackson Five.

  SUMMARY: Traces the career of the Jackson Five from their
start in Gary, Indiana, to their rise to the top of the recording
industry.
  1. Jackson 5 (Musical group) [1. Jackson 5
(Musical group) 2. Musicians. 3. Afro-Americans—
Biography] I. Title.
ML421.J3M36   784'.092'2 [B] [920] LC 76-11634
  ISBN 0-672-52148-2

186

*For my mother, Mrs. Margaret Manning,
and for the entire Jackson family,
without whom this book would not
have been possible*

Marlon, Joseph, Randy, LaToya, Mother Katherine, Jackie, Maureen, Tito, Michael. In front, Maureen's daughter, Stacy Ann, and Janet.

CONTENTS

FOREWORD

Musical groups in the United States come and go like the seasons. But once in a while a group will come along and capture the imagination of the country and absolutely thrill its audiences in a way that few entertainers can. When these groups come along, they also change, in many respects, the way in which music is performed. Over the last two decades, four groups stand out for this kind of musical achievement and its resulting influence on popular music. They are the Beatles, the Rolling Stones, the Supremes, and the Jacksons.

The Beatles took superior musicianship, fused it with American folk blues, and captivated an audience that ranged from the very young teeny boppers to the musical sophisticates in the classical genre. The Rolling Stones, in turn, reflected the pulse of the turned-on generation with their raunchy lyrics and daring visual presentation. The Supremes, backed by Motown, brought the ultimate in sophistication to rhythm and blues, bringing it from the honky-tonks in black neighborhoods to the American public with a glamour and glitter that made it finally acceptable.

But popular music had, for years, been geared directly to adults and young adults. The performers were nearly always adults, the producers were adults, and so were the people who decided what America was going to hear and see on television, the most important medium for launching new talent. And then came the Jackson Five.

They were called everything from "those kids from Gary" to practitioners of "bubble-gum soul." No matter. What they accomplished was to bring the music to the people who were doing the most to support the popular music industry in America— teenagers and sub-teenagers. What Leonard Bernstein was trying to accomplish in classical music the Jackson Five were doing in soul music. Their appeal was to the young. Wherever they went, young people flocked in large numbers to their concerts. Black and white, boys and girls—all could appreciate these musicians who were no older than they were, and perhaps even younger.

Michael Jackson was only eleven years old when he joined the group. Marlon was two years older, and the other members of the talented Jackson family ranged only a few years apart. Yet this was not a novelty group; the members of the Jackson Five were good musicians and superior showmen. Their rise to success was spectacular, but it came about only after years of training and dedication.

This is the story of the Jackson Five—of their training and successes, of the struggle of the Jackson family to keep the boys interested, and of their coping with the fruits and difficulties of success at a very young age. Moreover, it's a picture, a feeling, of what it is like to be world-famous as a teenager, doing something that you love, making music for the youth of the world.

FOREWORD

Marlon

"It's funny, but some people think we're so different from other young people. They'll see us in the lobby of a hotel buying some toothpaste and they'll say something like, 'Oh, do you brush your teeth?'

"What I like, other than performing, is being with my family. It's even nice being with my brothers when we're just sitting around the house with nothing to do. Sometimes we play a little basketball, or Tito will be taking his pictures. He takes a lot of pictures.

"People used to ask if we ever went to school. We were making a lot of records and appearances, but we still had to go to school. When we were too busy to go to school, we used to have a teacher who traveled with us. How about that? We'd get up and go to rehearsal and then we'd go back to the hotel room and study. It's a state law that entertainers have to get a certain amount of tutoring.

"The nicest thing about really doing well with the Jackson Five is that it's a family thing. You can always look back and know that whatever you did, you did with your own family. Everybody pitched in and helped. Back home in Gary we had a lot of chores to do, and we'd get everything done before we could practice. Now it's a lot easier, because we can afford help. But we still do most of the things that we were taught when we lived in Gary.

"Randy, our little brother, is the luckiest. After all, he's got five older brothers to help him do his homework.

"I still get excited when I see the top stars. People like Marvin Gaye, Diana Ross, the Temptations. They

really turn me on. The hardest thing to do is not to copy them. You see someone doing something, and if you really like the way they do it, you have a tendency to copy them. When we first started out we learned a lot by copying others, but now I think we have our own sounds and our own style.

"Sometimes I see other groups copying us. That's probably a mistake, because people realize what's going on.

"The fact that we're different ages is really good. We're a lot alike in many ways, but we're different because we are different ages and because no two people are ever alike. Everybody has his own idea of how to do things. It'd really be dull if we were just alike.

"I would like to be a professional dancer one day. I love dancing. I could dance all day if they let me. But then the rest of the Jackson Five have to get into the routine, too. You know what's really great? Being able to make a living doing what you love to do."

THE ROOTS

It began at 2300 Jackson Street in Gary, Indiana. The family of Joseph Jackson lived in a small two-bedroom house some miles from the heart of the city. The city itself had grown helter-skelter around the large industrial companies that processed steel and manufactured heavy machinery. Joseph Jackson worked in one of the mills, operating one of the giant cranes that lifted the heavy steel from place to place. It was a good life. Sometimes the monotony of it got to be a drag, but it was a way to support his growing family.

Joe Jackson worried a lot about his family. It wasn't that they weren't doing well, or at least as well as most black families in Gary. It was what was going on around them that kept him concerned. When he passed through Gary in the evenings, he could see young men standing around on the street corners or in little groups in front of the candy stores. Too often they had no jobs or anything at all to keep them occupied. Occasionally he would see them

[1]

Marlon takes a helicopter ride over New York City.

standing, half-bent and nodding, in the telltale stance of a junkie. There was a time when there weren't any junkies in Gary, but that time had long since passed. Now there was a drug problem, a crime problem, and every other kind of problem that he could possibly have imagined. His daughter had

grown up in this city, in the same house, but things had been a bit different then. With just the one child and, later, the baby to worry about, it was easy to keep them out of trouble. Even when the boys were younger he hadn't worried so. He had told himself that they were good boys and wouldn't get involved

[2]

in the gangs or the petty crime that seemed so much a part of life in a black community.

But he had also known children of friends who grew up and got into trouble—trouble with the police, trouble with drugs, trouble that ruined their lives and broke the hearts of their parents. It wouldn't be enough that the boys were from a "good" family; he had to encourage them in ways that would give each of them a strong image of himself—an image strong enough to resist the urge to wipe it out, an image that would carry each of them as far as his intelligence and abilities would allow.

Figuring out how to do this, though, was a lot more difficult than he had imagined. His job didn't offer much in the way of help. He couldn't very well have them operating a crane around the backyard. He didn't want them to, either. It was not that he had anything against being a crane operator. It was just that being a crane operator was something he had *had* to do. He didn't choose it as his life's work. He had had to do it because he had a family to provide for. He wanted his children to have something that few black children have—the opportunity to choose what they want to do with their lives.

Tito had a knack for putting things together. He was always making a cart or wagon of some sort. Perhaps Joe could encourage him in that. If the boy really was interested, he could be a mechanic, or even an engineer. He would be proud to have one of his sons become an engineer.

He realized that he couldn't neglect his wife, either. Katherine had been a blessing. She had

[3]

Michael with the author.

helped hold the family together when things had been roughest. She worked as a cashier and sales-woman to help with the family's expenses, and still did most of the work in maintaining the house. The boys chipped in, too, of course. Jermaine and Tito delivered newspapers in the neighborhood, and each of the boys had chores to do every day. Joe wouldn't tolerate any complaining to their mother when she told them to do something. They com-plained among themselves constantly, he thought, but it wasn't really serious. They really seemed to enjoy one another's company. That was a big plus for them, and made it somewhat easier for their mother.

Katherine was a deeply religious woman. She was devoted to both her church work and her family, seeing little difference in her work for either. Years before, when Joe had tried his luck in show business, she had not altogether approved of some of the places he had worked in, but she had still supported his efforts. He had played with a group, and they used to practice in the living room. Some of the players were surprised at Katherine's patience as they dragged their instruments and amplifiers into her living room. Katherine and Joe Jackson both realized, however, that they were just bringing into the home something that Joe loved very much and wanted very much to do. The group was good, but even good groups seldom make more than bare expenses, and sometimes not even that. Joe's group was no excep-tion.

The kids used to like the music, though. They'd sit around and listen to the group playing until their mother herded them off to bed. Sometimes, when the group wasn't at the Jackson home, the boys would pretend they were practicing, making the sounds of the instruments with their mouths and strumming away on make-believe guitars.

Tito had expressed an interest in his father's guitar, which stood in its case in the hall closet. The boy was much too young for a real guitar, especially an electric guitar, which required amplifiers and other electrical equipment. However, Joe and Katherine decided that they would include a guitar among the holiday presents that year. Tito took to it immediately, strumming the plastic strings furiously as he sang to anyone who would listen. He couldn't usually find a brother or sister who would actually sit down and listen to him, but he could always find one willing to beat on a box drum or pretend to be a saxophone. It didn't bother Tito that his brothers wouldn't listen to him; he couldn't play anyway. Not yet.

When Joe saw his son spending long hours on his toy guitar, he decided that he would encourage the boy by giving him lessons. He showed him how to tune the little guitar as well as it could be tuned, and taught him a few simple chords. Tito played them day and night. After a while his playing began to sound pretty good, even on the toy guitar.

His father wan't the only one who noticed his improvement. His brothers did as well, and they wanted to play the guitar, too. And if not the guitar, at least something.

Joe explained to his sons that playing music wasn't simply a matter of learning a few things. It meant a lot of work to really be able to play well.

When they were young, the boys had seen Joe's group practice for hours, and still nothing had come of it. But the boys insisted that they wanted to learn to play.

"It's only natural," Katherine had said when Joe told her that the boys wanted to play instruments. "They've seen you play, and we've always had some kind of music in the house."

Joe didn't want to promise the boys anything he couldn't deliver. Instruments cost money, and with a family the size of the Jacksons, money was not something that grew on trees.

"If you think they really want it, honey," Katherine said, reading the concern in her husband's face, "we'll make a way. With God's help, we'll make a way."

Making a way was easier said than done. It wasn't simply a matter of going downtown to the nearest music store and selecting instruments. It was scrimping and saving pennies here and there until the guitars and instruments the boys wanted were finally obtained. It meant fixing up old equipment and changing it to fit the new stuff that they bought. Often it meant going without other things that the boys or Joe and Katherine wanted, and using the money to buy a microphone or other equipment.

And it meant work, too. Joe was determined that the sacrifices the whole family had made were not going to go down the drain because the boys lacked interest. And it meant, for him, almost two full-time jobs.

He realized that for the boys to maintain their interest, they would have to see steady progress and that the progress would be largely up to him. Every evening after he came home from the mill, he would begin thinking about the boys' music and what they would practice that evening. He insisted that the whole family have dinner together each night and that there be no fooling around while they ate. He would check with Katherine to make sure that the chores she had assigned them had been done, as well as their homework. Then, when the dishes were done, they would start practice.

At first he would just teach them the fundamentals—how to play with each other, how to hit the right notes, and how to keep in time. The boys were impatient, but Joe insisted that they would not just become musicians—they would become *good* musicians. When they had mastered the basic parts of the music, he began teaching them the latest recordings of popular "Motown" groups, such as the Temptations.

Motown Records in Detroit had originated what became known as the Motown sound—a rich blend of melodic voices pushing a song through a driving but danceable rhythm. The Motown concept had borrowed from the doo-waah and a cappella groups of the fifties, but had added sophisticated orchestration, choreography, and costumes.

Slowly but surely the Jackson family's music-making evolved into more than just music. It became a show-business act. Joe Jackson would go to as many of the professional acts as he could to learn the dance steps that the groups were using. He would then come home and teach them to his boys. He tried different arrangements of voices and instruments,

A basketball game for charity.

The Jacksons with musical conductor Larry Farrow at the basketball game.

Michael.

looking for one that was at the same time professional and unique.

Nothing had been mentioned in the Jackson household to suggest that the boys would attempt to make a career out of their act. Joe Jackson knew that many youngsters, both black and white, had talent, but very few ever earned more than the applause of their family members for their efforts. He was determined that the Jackson family would not allow themselves to dream too big, too soon.

A high point in their training was when Mrs. Jackson measured the boys for costumes. "If you're going to sing the songs that the other groups do, you might as well look nice, too," she had said.

Measuring and making five costumes for the growing boys wasn't easy; neither was getting the money for the material and finding the time. But again, it was her family, and they were staying out of trouble. That was what counted.

The Jackson boys, who a few short months before could be found outside playing basketball or football, were now devoted stay-at-homes. They still had to do their homework and help out around the house, and the daily practice their father demanded left little room for anything else. But their practice was paying off. They sounded pretty good, at least to themselves, as they sat around a tape recorder listening to one of the practice sessions their father had taped. The only trouble was that, even though their friends and parents enjoyed their singing and dancing, they weren't sure how others would react to it—that is, until the school announced a talent contest.

THE ROOTS

Roosevelt High School in Gary is a predominantly black school. In Roosevelt, whatever you did you had to be good at, or the kids would get on you in a minute. The basketball team was one of the best in the city. In Indiana, where most of the schools have excellent basketball teams, this was an accomplishment. But besides the basketball team, there was a lot of other talent as well. Many of the kids could sing, and some of them were seriously considering becoming professionals. Their goal was to one day sign up with Motown Records in Detroit.

The competition at Roosevelt was keen. After each act the student audience would applaud as much as they felt appropriate for the act. For anyone who hasn't had the benefit of attending a talent contest in a black theater or school, the proceedings can appear a bit brutal. If an act is not liked, there is no polite applause at the end. Instead, the act is booed without pity. Sometimes the act isn't even allowed to finish before being booed off the stage. In New York's Apollo Theater, for example, when the audience is really displeased, the act is unceremoniously escorted off stage—usually for its own good! Just getting up on the stage of the Apollo to perform takes more nerve than most people have.

As the Jackson boys waited for their turn on stage, their stomachs began to turn. It was one thing to play and dance for your friends, who wanted to like you, but it was another thing entirely to perform in public for people who would just as soon boo as applaud. There was laughter out front when one of the acts, also a singing group, had a false start. When they started to sing, though, they were good. Finally it

[12]

was the Jacksons' turn. They had adopted the name the Jackson Five, and now the announcer was calling them onto the stage.

Joe Jackson tried to be as calm as possible as he wished them luck and told them to do the best they could. They had already set up their equipment, and they quickly went out to the middle of the stage. Tito rubbed his hands together, trying to remember not to wipe the sweaty palms on his costume. They were sweaty, though, and he was very nervous.

Out in the audience Mrs. Jackson sat waiting for the boys to begin. It was against her principles to pray for the boys to win, but she wanted so badly for them to do well that she almost did.

They began to sing. It was an arrangement of a Temptations song called "My Girl." The talk and shuffling of feet that had been constant during the other acts quieted down quickly. The audience was at first stunned into silence by the highly polished

THE JACKSONS

group. And then they came alive. For all intents and purposes, the talent show was over, and the Jackson Five had taken over the stage.

Michael Jackson was singing lead. He was much younger than the students at Roosevelt High, but he had captured them. Soon the whole audience was swaying to the rock-steady beat and magic of the Jackson Five. They won the trophy for first place in the talent contest, and, even more important, they had established that they were a musical group that people loved. For the Jackson Five, the inexpensive trophy was just the beginning.

Randy, Jackie, Michael and Marlon with actress Nora Aunor.

Tito

"It's funny, but when I'm on the stage performing and the audience is listening to what we're doing and watching us, I'm also watching the audience and listening to them. That's the best part of being with the Jackson Five. When the audience really starts to get carried away, it's fantastic.

"And when girls scream, it just knocks me right out. People who aren't in entertainment don't realize sometimes that the people performing are getting just as much of a kick as the people watching. I can see Michael and Jermaine respond to the audience, too. A show will be so-so; maybe we're really tired. Near the end of a tour, you're always tired. The show will be dragging along a little, and all of a sudden the audience will start clapping or shouting, and Michael will respond right away. We all respond.

"I would like my children to be in a group like the Jackson Five, if they're willing to work hard enough to make themselves really good and if they can be as happy as we were. We weren't pushed into it; it was something that we enjoyed and were willing to work for.

"I think everyone should have one chance to get up in front of an audience and do his thing. Some people wouldn't dig it, I know. Some entertainers don't even dig it. They act as if they have to force themselves to perform every time. Then they end up becoming back-up singers or musicians and just recording in studios and that kind of thing.

"But I love it. It's really exciting, and I'm glad I'm part of it. I realize that a lot of people–most people in fact–won't ever have the chance.

"I'm pretty much a perfectionist. I want things to be right. If I'm working on a number, I want to play it as well as I can. I think I got that from my parents. You know, when we were starting out, all I heard were things like 'You owe it to yourself to be as much as you can.'

"I want to be the best musician and entertainer that I can be. And now that I'm married, I want to be the best husband and the best father I can be, too. If I do anything else, I'll want to be the best at that, too."

FORMING
THE GROUP

Tito was playing lead guitar during the early days of the group, having graduated from the Sears, Roebuck toy guitar that he had started on. The guitar was a leftover from Joseph Jackson's old days with his own group, the Falcons, as was most of the equipment used by the new vocal group. A second-hand bass guitar was bought for Jermaine when funds became available.

Family friend Johnny Jackson owned and played a set of drums, and another friend, Ronnie Rancifer, accompanied on the keyboard. They were still playing arrangements that Joseph Jackson had written after listening to other soul groups. Jermaine, who was impressed by Motown recording star Stevie Wonder, was also doubling as lead vocalist when the group first began.

Michael didn't join the group until he was six, and Marlon joined shortly thereafter. They played wherever anyone would let them, usually for free or, occasionally, for enough money to cover transporta-

(At left) *Randy on shopping spree on London's Kings Road.*

tion. With Michael and Marlon in the group, the act consisted mainly of dancing to an already popular record. Michael copied much of the choreography of James Brown, the "Godfather of Soul." One of his favorite tricks was to hold the microphone in front of him as he sang, release it, and spin around and catch it before it fell.

"It used to fall a lot when I first started doing it," Michael said, "but after a while I got the hang of it and wouldn't even have to think about it."

And of course Joseph Jackson made sure that his son didn't do it in public until he had mastered it.

Actually, the boys were entertaining themselves as much as they were entertaining others. The hard work getting all the routines down was worth it as they began to hear the way they sounded. They thought they sounded good, and more and more their audiences were telling them the same thing by their applause and enthusiasm. Slowly they began to give up other things to devote more time to their music. Jackie, who loved football, played less and less. Michael abandoned many of his friends to spend time with the group. They couldn't give up their entire lives for the group, but sometimes the things they had to give up weren't that desirable.

"Gary was okay," Jackie said. "We lived in a nice area and everything, but there were a lot of things around that weren't too cool. You know, different ways you could get into trouble. When I'd want to go to a party or something, I always had to be home at a certain time and let my parents know where the party was and everything. If it didn't sound right, then I couldn't go.

Signing autographs in front of Buckingham Palace.

In Las Vegas.

"Sometimes I'd get a little mad, but what really made it for me, and for all of us, was that our music was so positive. We were doing something we liked a lot and it was keeping us out of trouble, and it was groovy, too. I saw some other guys that didn't make it. Some of them got hung up into drugs and what have you. So what can you say when your parents do something, lead you someplace where you make it? You've got to be thankful."

If it was rough before the triumph at Roosevelt High, it became even rougher afterward. The Jackson Five began to appear at theaters around Gary and in nearby Chicago. In Chicago they appeared at the Regal Theater on the same program with Smokey Robinson and the Miracles. Joseph Jackson booked the group and acted as chaperon, manager, trainer, and stagehand for the boys. The appearance with the Miracles was the biggest program that the young group had participated in. Later they made appearances in places as far away as New York's Apollo Theater.

"When we heard we were going to the Apollo, it was really something else," Michael said, reliving the excitement. "We went around talking about everybody who had appeared at the Apollo and everything. You know, all the big names have been there. James Brown, the Temptations, Ella Fitzgerald, the Supremes. Everybody!

"The only thing that was different for us was how we got there. We had this Volkswagen bus, and we all got in the back with the equipment and everything, and off we went. It's not such a long trip if you fly—in fact, it's really short—but if you have to ride in the back of a little truck like that, it's kind of rough.

"And another thing. When the Miracles or some group like that finish their engagement, they either fly back home and have their manager check out their equipment and costumes, or they check into a hotel or something. We would just load ourselves and our stuff back onto the bus and come home. It was exciting, but sometimes I'd be so tired I couldn't even see straight. Once, we got back home just about in time to change and go to school. I'd be sitting up in school dreaming about the Apollo."

In addition to performing in such theaters as the Apollo in New York and the Uptown in Philadelphia, the Jackson Five continued to enter talent contests. In the early days they amassed more trophies winning contests than they accumulated money. Sometimes the money they made, even in a large, well-known theater, wasn't even enough to cover their expenses. They had to eat on the road, replace equipment that wore out, get their costumes cleaned and cared for, and maintain the old blue VW.

They began to learn what life was like on the road. It wasn't as glamorous as they had imagined it would be. Sometimes on a weekend they would have to appear at several theaters in different cities and would end up catching what little sleep they could on the road. Their father and family friend Jack Richardson took turns driving. They learned that it didn't matter how tired they were or how many times they had performed the same song; the fans wanted to hear them at their best. Often they wouldn't feel at their best, and it was during these times that the long hours of practice paid off. They knew their music so well that they could play it no matter how tired they felt. They also discovered that, long after the audience had left, they would often still be in the theater packing up their equipment to go to the next town to do the same show over again. If they were going to be conceited, several weekends on the road would soon change their outlook.

"Sometimes we would stay in a hotel or a motor inn, and we'd wake up and not even know where we were," Tito said. "Even though a few hours earlier the fans were screaming for you, the people in the hotel wouldn't even know who you were.

"You start thinking to yourself that maybe it's not so good after all, especially when you see the hotel bill and you figure out you didn't even make enough money to cover the bill. My father was still working, and a lot of his money from his job went to help support the group, and my mother was still doing sewing for us and making sure that our costumes were nice and everything. So it really wasn't easy. When we got a week at the Apollo during Christmas, we stayed with friends, and still the money was so tight I didn't even want to ask for a hamburger or anything. And as much as we thought we knew before, we were learning more every day."

The Jackson Five's first recording was with a small company in Gary called Steel Town Records. Their first record was a single called "Big Boy." It went over fairly well locally. They also cut another single called "You Don't Have to Be Twenty-One to Fall in Love." It was their first real studio experience and yet another phase for the rapidly maturing group.

Jermaine

"One of the things about being with the Jackson Five is the traveling. Sometimes it's really hard, and you have to force yourself to make the effort to pack your stuff and get ready for the next town.

"I think that's the difference between being a professional and being an amateur. When we were playing around Gary, we'd just have to go across town or take a short ride to get home. But when we started playing in other cities, we'd find ourselves on the road all night and get home just in time to go to school.

"You see life differently when you're traveling around a lot. You find out that people are really pretty much the same. We'd be in New York, say, and the people would like us, and then we'd go to California and we'd be nervous, but we'd find out that the people liked the same things in California that they did in New York. Also, we found out how nice people can be. When you're away from home and you stop in a restaurant to get breakfast and someone gives you a nice cheery hello, it makes you feel good. People respond to you if you treat them with respect.

"The most interesting place we've been, at least for me, was Africa. I didn't realize how many wrong impressions I had of Africa. If I'd gone over there and had seen people standing around in those little

[25]

loincloths or what have you, I wouldn't have been surprised. That's what the movies and television had taught me, and what I read in the history books in school. You read about Africa and all you see is a picture of white people taking some slaves to a ship, or black people carrying bundles for some white explorer.

"I was really surprised to see modern cities and buildings–some of them better looking than a lot I've seen in this country.

"We went to Gorée Island to see the old slave fort, and all this was something new to me. All of Africa was new to me. Because the Africa I had heard about and read about seemed so foreign to the way that I was, I guess I rejected it. But when I saw what Africa was, what it really was, I was impressed. It's a beautiful continent. And when I looked into the faces of the people, black people, I felt good because I was looking into my own heritage for the first time.

"Traveling with the Jackson Five gave me an opportunity to see Africa, and if I never travel anywhere else, it will have been worth it for that one opportunity."

Tito, Joseph, Jackie, Randy, Jermaine, Marlon and Michael at Gorée Island's Slave Castle.

Randy.

Arrival at Dakar.

On Gorée Island, where slaves were once traded.

Concert promoter Johnny Secka and the Jacksons are shown leg shackles worn by slaves at the Gorée Island prison.

Michael Jackson and Jackie in Senegal.

Michael and friends.

Marlon in Senegal.

Jackie at the Gorée Island marketplace.

Randy with a Nigerian student in Senegal.

Michael and Randy with guide in Senegal and (below) with Nigerian students.

(Below) Michael listens as Gruit (oral historian) explains how slaves were quartered prior to shipment to the New World.

THE RISE
TO THE TOP

As the popularity of the group grew, they received many offers to sign recording contracts. Joe Jackson had enough experience in the entertainment industry to be careful about signing a contract for the Jackson Five. Motown, in Detroit, was the biggest company in the business dealing exclusively with soul music. It was with a Motown recording artist, Diana Ross, that the Jackson Five began the string of successes that would eventually bring them worldwide fame.

Diana Ross introduced the group to the public. She had heard about them from Gary mayor Richard Hatcher. She was delighted with the group, recognizing their freshness and their instant appeal. She recommended the group to Motown president Berry Gordy, Jr., who had already heard good things about them. Soon, a seven-year contract was signed. The Jackson Five were Motown stars!

At one time, a listener could distinguish between white and black recording artists by the quality of the arrangements and the technical competence of the recording studios. Black groups with good singing voices were often hampered by the production of lusterless recordings and poor arrangements. White companies, by and large, simply produced better records. To a great extent, Motown turned this around. The Motown sound was marked by superior recordings, both artistically and technically speaking, and by an overall professionalism that extended even to the appearance of the record jackets. Each Motown artist was carefully groomed to achieve his full potential.

When the Jackson Five came to Motown, it was decided that they would develop their own distinctive style and drop many of the things which were readily identifiable as being borrowed from other singers or groups. Their signing with Motown signaled to the entertainment world that the Jackson Five had arrived! Few realized at the time what an impact that arrival would make.

In 1969 the group made their first network television appearance on the Miss Black Teenage American pageant emceed by radio and TV personality Hal Jackson.

"Yeah, we were nervous," Tito said. "You get used to working with an audience, and you can respond. If the audience likes what you're doing, you know it and you can keep it going. In other words, you know that the people you're supposed to be entertaining like what you're doing.

"Television is something else, though. You don't know what people are thinking about while they're

[36]

watching you. They could be sitting in their living rooms eating salami sandwiches and not even paying you any mind, or they could be clapping their hands and getting into the music. You can never tell. You just see that little red light and you know that somebody's watching. The best thing to do, I guess, is just try to ignore it."

They appeared with Diana Ross and the Supremes on ABC television, from the Hollywood Palace. People were beginning to notice the Jackson Five, and they were beginning to get star treatment.

"People started recognizing us on the street,"

The Jacksons greet Ms. U.S. Talented Teen.

Marlon, LaToya, and Randy.

Tito says, "and they'd say, 'Hey, there goes that group the Jackson Brothers,' and things like that. Sometimes people wouldn't even really know who we were, but they'd ask for our autographs because other people were asking us."

The top music charts are the ones found in *Billboard, Record World,* and *Cash Box.* In the beginning of 1970 the Jackson Five were at the top of all three of them. They began to sell records by the millions; their first album, *Diana Ross Presents the Jackson Five,* received the coveted gold record for a million dollars in sales, and eventually received a platinum record for actually selling a million copies.

[38]

The Jacksons accept an award from radio station WNJR in
Newark, New Jersey.

Jermaine.

"A-B-C," a single release, sold more than two million copies. Almost overnight the Jackson Five were a smashing success. At first it was thought that they appealed chiefly to black youngsters, but it was soon discovered that they appealed to people all over the country, regardless of race and with little regard to age. The group that had entertained the elderly just for a place to play and try out their material was having even more success entertaining young people. Their success was the most amazing ever. Even the Beatles had not caught on as rapidly.

Ed Sullivan had them on his show and was completely captivated not only by their musical ability, but by the fact that the boys were both polite and charming.

"Remember," he said to Michael, "to thank God for your talent every day."

In June they started their first national tour. At the Cow Palace in San Francisco they grossed $75,000. At the Los Angeles Forum a few days later the gross was over $175,000.

Meanwhile, they released The Love You Save and the single "I'll Be There." They had released four singles since reaching Motown, and all four had hit the very top of the charts.

When "Never Can Say Goodbye" was released, their fans and the record stores around the country were eager for it. It sold more than a million copies in less than a week.

Jermaine tells what their new success was like:

"At first it was so exciting we couldn't keep up with what was going on. Wherever we went, people

[41]

At Radio City Music Hall.

Michael with Nora Aunor, movie actress.

would recognize us and point us out. Girls would send little love letters to us. It was very nice. During that first tour we hit forty cities in sixty days. You learn a lot. You learn how cities are different and how to get around and things like that.

A TYPICAL JACKSON FIVE TOUR

August 3	Richmond, Virginia
August 4	Hampton, Virginia
August 5	Baltimore, Maryland
August 7	Greensboro, North Carolina
August 8	Nashville, Tennessee
August 10	Columbia, South Carolina
August 11	Atlanta, Georgia
August 12	Miami, Florida
August 17	Memphis, Tennessee
August 18	St. Louis, Missouri
August 21	New Orleans, Louisiana
August 22	Dallas, Texas
August 24	San Francisco, California
August 25	Los Angeles, California
August 26	Las Vegas, Nevada
September 2	Honolulu, Hawaii

"Then you start reading about yourself. And that's kind of hard to take. People say that you're this and you're that, and instead of thinking that what you're doing is great, you begin to think that *you're* great. And that can be a trap. Because if *you're* great, then all you have to do is just walk out on the stage and everything's fine and everybody's going to love you. If what you're *doing* is great, then you have to work at it to keep it that way. Some entertainers begin to believe that they're so great that all they have to do is walk out and say, 'Here I am.' But it really doesn't work that way. Every time we started to get a little too much for ourselves, our father and mother would remind us of how hard we worked to get where we were. That always brought us back down to earth.

"Then, after a while, things get to be work. You know, it's hard to do a show or two, and even three shows a day, and then pack up your stuff and split to the next town. That's really hard work. In Gary it was pretty easy because when we finished practicing or playing in town, all we had to do was go home and go to bed. Sometimes, as a professional, you have to do your shows and then head right out to the airport to get to the next town. And people don't want to hear that you're tired. That's not what they're paying their money for."

At the end of the summer, when the tour was completed, they had grossed 4.5 million dollars, more money than they had made in their entire professional lives before the tour. After the last day of the tour they were back in school.

The tour was over, but the money kept pouring in. There were Jackson Five books, Jackson Five posters, Jackson Five anything you could get a picture or lettering on. Fred Rice, who handled the rights of the Beatles and the Monkees, handled their licensing, the rights for a manufacturer to use their names and pictures on his product.

When the Jackson Five returned to Gary, they were given the key to the city. Later, they were honored by both the U.S. Senate and the House of Representatives. They had changed, and so had Gary. The little town they had come from was just not the same for them. It was a place that lacked the excitement and glamour they had come to know. They still loved Gary and its people, but they decided to buy a home in California. The struggling Jackson family was now on the verge of being wealthy.

Michael

"The hardest thing is knowing what people are really like. My father used to warn us that a lot of people would pretend to like us, but they really wouldn't care one way or the other. They'd like us as a musical group or they'd like the way we danced, but they wouldn't really have a chance to get to know us, so they really couldn't like us personally.

"But we'd be someplace, and people would come up to us and speak and be pleasant, and maybe they'd tell me that they liked me as a person, as Michael. But I really think they liked me as part of the Jackson Five. It might not seem like a big problem, but it can be one sometimes. Now, I know that my brothers and my parents like me, and I have friends who I'm pretty tight with. That's all cool, but do you

[45]

know how many people I meet? Sometimes I meet so many people on a tour that they all start to look the same and sound the same and even seem to say the same thing.

"I like people. I see somebody who's kind of friendly looking, and I really like that person. But there are some people I really don't care for, and I just try to avoid them.

"What I really don't want to be is phony with people. I see some entertainers who smile at people and the moment the people walk away they begin to bad-mouth them. I don't ever want to be like that.

"Sometimes people make demands on you that really put you uptight. Maybe you're tired from traveling all night and all you want to do is get into bed, and people want you to stop and sign autographs and things like that. You'd be surprised what people want you to autograph, too. Anyway, you just about have to do it because they're your fans and all. If you don't have them, you don't have anything.

"Getting along with people when you're an entertainer, when you're pretty popular like the Jackson Five, is important. You have to remember who you are. You're an entertainer and you can do something that other people can't do. But at the same time that you're different, you're not so different that you're better than anyone else. Does that make sense?

"I don't know of anything more exciting than being a member of the group. It's what I've done since I was eleven. One day I'd like to act or perhaps direct movies. Something involved with a lot of people."

[47]

(At left)   *Michael.*

THE MATURING GROUP

The problems of a group like the Jackson Five are very different from those of most people their ages. When success comes as early in life as it has for the dynamic singing group, the problems come equally early. Instead of trying to figure out how to conduct one's life to reach goals that will lead to a happy life, the Jackson Five were presented with the problem of how to deal with the success they already had.

Early in life there were pressures to work together and to form a group. These pressures came from the need to stay out of trouble and to find some outlet for their talents. There was also the great love of family which they all shared and which helped them through their years of struggle to perfect their talents. Now, as they seem to "have it made," there are other pressures that begin to pull at the group.

The first pressure is their commercial success. Things that they had done for fun as youngsters, they are now being paid for. The group makes a great deal of money, in the millions of dollars. Producers and

Janet and Randy.

companies who initially saw the Jackson Five as just another group that could fill in some spot on a program now see them as a source of high revenues. Producers, manufacturers, and people in and out of show business hound them daily to get the group to appear here or there or to get them to endorse products. The name and pictures of the Jackson Five on T-shirts are worth thousands of dollars. Many people approach them with honest business deals, and many try to exploit them. People have even invited them to parties and then asked them to entertain for nothing. The group has had to hire people to protect them against those who want to use them, their name, or their pictures without permission. It has become so bad that anytime someone approaches a member of the group, it is necessary to avoid all discussion of any kind of business deal and to send the person to their managers or attorneys.

[50]

THE JACKSONS

The Jackson Five realize that they have a responsibility to the public and to their fans, and they don't mind that at all, but they don't want to be used to make money for other people or to be taken advantage of.

Many people love celebrities and see them as wonderful people who, like the Jackson Five, can be very entertaining and bring happiness or amusement. On the other hand, some resent the success of others very much, and it's not unusual for someone to deliberately pick a fight with a member of the group or try to do something to harm one of the members. People often forget, too, that the group is not made up of plastic people who sing and dance. They are normal people who have worked very hard to get where they are and have normal desires and needs. If one of the group is at dinner with his girl friend, for example, he might not mind stopping once to sign an autograph, but he will probably re-

sent it if his entire dinner is ruined by people asking him to sign slips of paper or asking questions about the group. His girl friend will probably resent it, too.

The Jackson Five have realized that there is a price to pay for their fame and the money they are making. They cannot be as friendly with everyone as they once were. They have to be careful whom they deal with and what they say. The fact that they want and need privacy the same as everyone else is often overlooked. Sometimes when people stop one of them and say, "Aren't you one of the Jackson Five?" they just look around and say, "Who, me?"

Another source of pressure within the group is the very fact that they are a *group*. Even though they love one another and their family, they are all maturing in slightly different ways. They all have individual interests, but they spend most of their time together. They travel together, practice together, and spend most of their waking hours being the Jackson Five instead of being Tito, Jackie, Michael, Jermaine, and Marlon. Being with the same people day in and day out for years is difficult, no matter how much you care for them. It becomes even more difficult when you are doing the same thing day after day!

The question came up whether or not the boys wanted to continue working together. Did they want to remain the Jackson Five, or did they want to do other things? The money they had made gave them options. They could have, if they had wanted to, started their own acts or even gone into different lines of work altogether. Michael had made some singles on his own, and they were successful. Jermaine too had made records, which also did well. The

[52]

temptation for individual members of the Jackson Five to make solo recordings was—and is—great. If a member of the group makes it on his own, then he has the freedom to develop independently of the group and according to his individual abilities.

On June 16, 1972, Tito Jackson got married. He was the first of the Jackson Five to marry and, subsequently, the first of the Jackson Five to become a father. Tito Adaryll Jackson II is the baby's name. Many people felt that Tito's marriage would be the beginning of the end of the Jackson Five. They felt that the young people the Jackson Five appealed to might not identify with the new "married" image. This proved to be very wrong, however, as young people became as interested in the marriage as they were in the professional careers of the group. Jermaine was the next to tie the knot, marrying Hazel Joy Gordy, the daughter of Motown president Berry Gordy, Jr., on December 15, 1973, in one of the most lavish celebrations in Hollywood history. When Jackie then married Enid Spann in November of 1974 that made Michael and Marlon the only bachelors left in the group. Marlon married Carol Parker of New Orleans on August 16, 1975, but did not reveal that he was married for quite some time.

It's interesting that the Jackson Five married at all. Many popular entertainers, aware that they can date as many girls as they want without the responsibilities involved with marriage, choose never to take the vows of matrimony. It is probably the strong family ties and the strong religious feeling within the family that prompted the boys to marry. But marriage has also added new burdens to the group. Now not

Randy.

only do the individual members of the group have to get along with one another, but they also have to leave their wives and families behind or, if they choose to have them travel with them, subject them to the same kind of pressures that the rest of the group experiences.

Many groups have made it and then broken up. The Supremes, one of the major Motown groups, broke up, for all intents and purposes, when Diana Ross left. There was still a group called the Supremes, but it had nowhere near the success of the group that contained the fabulous Miss Ross. Although Diana Ross is now a star in her own right, most groups that break up find that individual members cannot make it on their own. This is true even when the members of the group have made hit records while still with the group.

One group that broke up, the Beatles, has simply not had a strong desire to get back together again professionally. The fact that they made enough money not to need the income from the group has of course helped.

One last pressure on the group is the idea of artistic growth. Michael's appeal as a young boy changes as he matures. So do his interests. If he is to grow artistically, he must face his own maturing and his own changing tastes and adjust to them. This holds true for Jermaine, Tito, Marlon, and Jackie as well. The problem with not changing, of course, is that the public might well become tired of the same sound and the same act, no matter how smoothly it goes. The decline in the popularity of James Brown,

Randy.

for example, has been due largely to the sameness of his recordings and his act. The Godfather of Soul might well have done his thing once too often.

"I like being a member of the Jackson Five," Jermaine said, "but I also have to be me. I realize my responsibility to the Jackson Five, but I can't postpone what I'm all about forever, either."

Jackie

"I try to look forward. What do I want to do with my life? What kind of career do I want—that kind of thing. I've been interested in a lot of things: sports, cars, motorbikes. What I know best, of course, is entertainment.

[56]

THE JACKSONS

"There's more to the business than just being on stage. I'd like to produce records, perhaps for the Jackson Five, and then for other groups. When a show is put on, there are a lot of people involved other than the performers. Somebody has to rent the theater, somebody has to put up the money to book the acts, and somebody has to make the financial arrangements.

"I've taken courses at a business college in order to prepare myself to work in the management end of entertainment. You really have to have the right kind of education to understand the tricky financial aspects of this business.

"Money comes fairly easy when you've built up a string of successes, but it can go faster than it comes in if you're not careful. Some people think of entertainment as something you play around with, but actually it's a job. Hey, it's a glamorous job. Right now I can't think of anything I'd rather be doing, but it is a job. It's how I support myself. People in show business who aren't properly educated have to rely on someone else to manage their financial affairs. It's not unusual to hear about someone you would think would really be over, and find out that they don't have a dime! I was surprised to find out that some big stars really aren't doing well financially.

"At one time I thought, Hey, I'm an entertainer and I don't really need a lot of schooling. I didn't go around saying it all the time, but that's how I felt. But the more I know about the business, the more I realize that to stay on top means more than just singing and dancing. I go to a business college in between

Jackie.

tours. It's funny in a way. I used to go to school when we were trying to become something, because I had to go. Now that we've had some success, I go to school because I realize what I need to get over.

"I think I can be creative in a business way as well as artistically. If I put the same amount of work into learning about business that I did into learning how to make music, I'll be okay."

THE JACKSONS

Jackie.

Jackie.

EPILOGUE

An interesting sidelight of Jermaine's marriage to Hazel Gordy, the daughter of Motown's Berry Gordy, Jr., is that Jermaine is still a Motown artist, while the other Jackson brothers have signed with Epic Records. Randy Jackson, the youngest of the boys, had already been rehearsing with the group, and started performing with them on a regular basis. Also joining the group were Janet Jackson, the youngest member of the family, LaToya, and Maureen, the eldest member of the Jackson family.

Randy and Janet began doing duets which were immediately a smash. The introduction of Janet, Maureen and LaToya to the group also added another dimension. The Jackson Five had previously consisted of all boys, which was a rather routine situation in show business. There are few mixed groups which have been successful. One of the most popular mixed groups is the Fifth Dimension, but their appeal is to an older audience than that of the Jacksons.

EPILOGUE

Maureen ♊

May 29, 1950
Gemini
Maureen Reilette Brown

LaToya ♊

May 29, 1956
Gemini
LaToya Yvonne

Jackie ♉

May 4, 1951
Taurus
Sigmund Esco

Marlon ♓

March 12, 1957
Pisces
Marlon David

Tito ♎

October 15, 1953
Libra
Toriano Adaryll

Michael ♍

August 29, 1958
Virgo
Michael Joe

Jermaine ♐

December 11, 1954
Sagittarius
Jermaine Lajuan

Randy ♏

October 29, 1962
Scorpio
Steven Randall

Janet ♉

May 16, 1966
Taurus
Janet Damita Jo

Randy and Janet.

EPILOGUE

With the introduction of the Jackson girls, the nature of the group changed from that of the usual male quintet to a family act. Not only did Janet and Randy perform together, but LaToya and Maureen added a completely new vocal range and a host of new possibilities for the choreographer. Instead of simply doing coordinated dance steps, the Jacksons are now doing complete routines reminiscent of Hollywood's Fred Astaire and Gene Kelly period.

Another benefit of having as many as eight members of the family on stage at a time is that the act can take on a much more sophisticated approach. With all of the Jacksons onstage, and with all of them displaying a versatility and talent rarely found in a family act, the possibilities become limitless. The CBS television network, the first one that the Jackson Five had appeared on nationally, did a series of specials called "The Jackson Family." The response to the CBS programs was overwhelming. Thousands of fans called the studio to find out if the programs would be continued. It was by far one of the highlights of the network's family entertainment efforts.

This new title, The Jackson Family, fit the new concept of having eight members very well. There was also some problem as to who owned the rights to the name "Jackson Five." Motown claimed that they owned the rights to the name despite the fact that the Jacksons had signed with another company. It's not unusual for a show-business act not to own the rights to the name it uses professionally.

The Jacksons are not the first family to be in show business, nor will they be the last. But they are one of the most talented groups to appear in many years.

[64]

THE JACKSONS

They are still a very young group, and, with their exceptional singing and dancing ability, one that will probably be bringing us a great deal of entertainment in the years to come.

Courtesy CBS Television